FIND THE ANIMAL

GOD MADE SOMETHING ENORMOUS

There is a big penguin, a middle sized penguin and a little penguin hidden in the pages of this book. Can you find them all?

PENNY REEVE

ILLUSTRATED BY ROGER DE KLERK

CF4•K

For Patrick

Are you ready for another adventure? Let's see what we can find. It's something God has made, and it's something enormous!

Can you see the little boat?

Love is patient. Love is kind. 1 Corinthians 13:4

Where is the biggest seagull?

Look at that! It's a tail. God gave this animal an enormous tail which it uses for swimming, dancing and showing off above the water!

Can you see a little dolphin?

Love rejoices in the truth.
1 Corinthians 13:6

Who has the biggest life jacket?

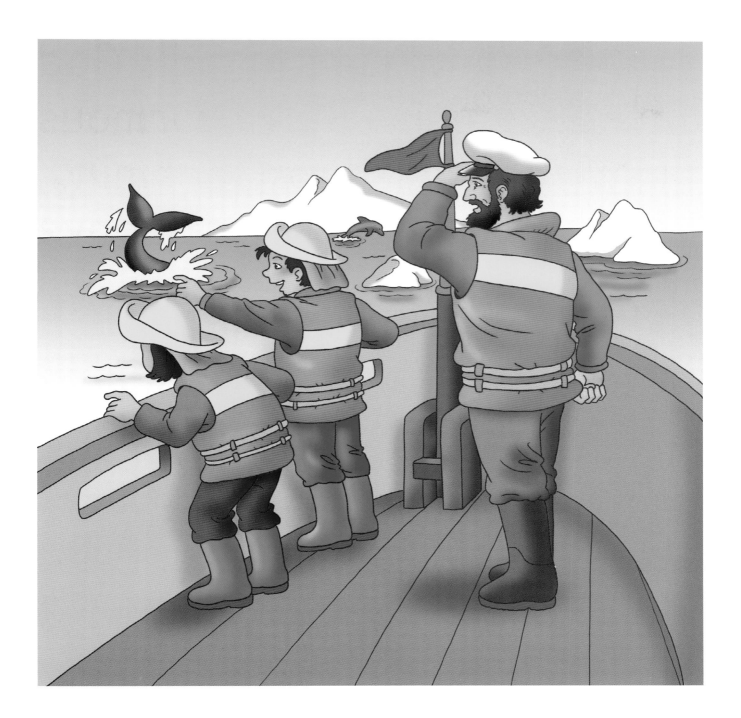

What's that? It's a fin. This animal doesn't have fingers and it doesn't have toes. God gave this animal enormous fins to help it swim through deep ocean waters.

Where is the largest flying fish?

Love never fails. 1 Corinthians 13:8

Point to the largest iceberg.

What might that be? It's an eye. God gave this enormous animal beautiful big eyes that sometimes come right up close and take a look at you.

Where is the little crab?

Love is not easily angered.
1 Corinthians 13:5

Who has the biggest fishing bucket?

Did you just get wet? This enormous animal uses a blow hole on the top of its head to breathe in air and shoot air and water out.

Can you see the little seal?

Love keeps no record of wrongs. 1 Corinthians 13:5

Where is the big seal?

Do you know which animal we've found? Yes, you're right. It's a whale. And who made it? Our great God!

What is bigger, the boat or the whale?

God is love. 1 John 4:16

Can you see two little birds?

Whales are the most enormous animals in the world today. But God's love is even more enormous than that! God doesn't wait for us to be any bigger or stronger or better before he loves us. He loves us just as we are.

What is the smallest animal on this page?

This is love: not that we loved God, but that he loved us.
1 John 4:10

What is the biggest animal?

Thank you, God, that I don't have to be bigger or smarter or faster for you to love me. Help me to come to you, just as I am, and trust in your enormous love.

"God demonstrates his love for us in this: while we were still sinners, Christ died for us." Romans 5:8